Mexican Jenny
and Other Poems

D1714789

ANHINGA PRESS

MEXICAN JENNY
AND OTHER POEMS

BARBARA BRINSON CURIEL

2012 Philip Levine
Prize for Poetry

Selected by Cornelius Eady

ANHINGA PRESS
TALLAHASSEE, FLORIDA 2014

Cover art: *Antique Quilt, circa 1886.*
            © Allen McDavid Stoddard/Shutterstock.com
Author photograph: Michael Twombly
Cover and text design: Carol Lynne Knight
Type Styles: titles and text set in Schneidler BT

Library of Congress Cataloging-in-Publication Data
Mexican Jenny and Other Poems by Barbara Brinson Curiel, First Edition
ISBN – 978-1-934695-36-4
Library of Congress Cataloging Card Number – 2013950667

Anhinga Press Inc. is a nonprofit corporation
dedicated wholly to the publication and appreciation
of fine poetry and other literary genres.

For personal orders, catalogs
and information write to:
Anhinga Press
P.O. Box 3665
Tallahassee, Florida 32315
Website: www.anhinga.org
E-mail: info@anhinga.org

Published in the United States
by Anhinga Press
Tallahassee, Florida
First Edition, 2014

For Allie and Alex,
and for Michael

THE PHILIP LEVINE PRIZE FOR POETRY

The annual competition for the Philip Levine Prize for Poetry is sponsored and administered by the M.F.A. Program in Creative writing at California State University, Fresno.

2012
Barbara Brinson Curiel
Mexican Jenny and Other Poems
Selected by Cornelius Eady

2011
Ariana Nadia Nash
Instructions for Preparing Your Skin
Selected by Denise Duhamel

2010
Lory Bedikian
The Book of Lamenting
Selected by Brian Turner

2009
Sarah Wetzel
Bathsheba Transatlantic
Selected by Garrett Hongo

2008
Shane Seely
The Snowbound House
Selected by Dorianne Laux

2007
Neil Aitken
The Lost Country of Sight
Selected by C.G. Hanzlicek

2006
Lynn Aarti Chandhok
The View from Zero Bridge
Selected by Corrinne Clegg Hales

2005
Roxane Beth Johnson
Jubilee
Selected by Philip Levine

2002
Steven Gehrke
The Pyramids of Malpighi
Selected by Philip Levine

2001
Fleda Brown
Breathing In, Breathing Out
Selected by Philip Levine

Contents

ACKNOWLEDGMENTS

I gratefully acknowledge the editors of the following journals, who published some of the poems in this collection:

The Acentos Review: "My Father Comes Home from Work"

Brother Jonathan Review: "Dinner with Julia,"
   "Immigrant's Pantoum"

El Corto: "Goldilocks"

Huizache: "Cuban Missile Crisis"

Kweli Journal: "Note to the Owner of the Restaurant
   Where My Daughter Works"

Pilgrimage: "Palm Reader," "Homecoming: San Francisco, 1965"

"7 Stanzas About Rum," appeared in the chapbook anthology
Mirage: New Poems, published by Bunchgrass Press.

I am also grateful to the CantoMundo poetry community for their fellowship, good advice, encouragement, and for the gift of being with mi gente.

Thank you also Red Shuttleworth, my first and best poetry teacher, now good friend, mentor poet, and source of inspiration and wisdom, who when I was thirteen years old in San Francisco, put me on the path by teaching me the measure of words.

MEXICAN JENNY
AND OTHER POEMS

Hay países, hay ríos,
en tus ojos,
mi patria está en tus ojos…
    — Pablo Neruda

FAMILY PICTURE

FAMILY PICTURE

I'm helping Ramona
find a place for her family
so she can move from Ohio to California
to take her new job at the university.

A landlord shows me
the one apartment I've seen
with a clean
kitchen stove

and then he calls Ramona
to request a picture
of her family
— *email is fine* —

so he'll know,
what kind
of people
they are.

Ramona tells him
she teaches about inequality and justice.
She tells him she worries
about prejudice.

Oh no, he says
with an immigrant's accent
I wasn't able to place,
I'm not prejudiced.

Just send the picture.

Immigrant's Pantoum

Fortunes scattered, broken glass across the threshold,
What wealth we had could be held in a palm.
So we took to the road one cold morning.
The path was hard, we didn't know the way.

What wealth we had could be held in a palm,
Hidden in a sack, an apron pocket.
The path was hard, we didn't know the way.
We looked to stars in our children's eyes for signs.

Hidden in a sack, an apron pocket,
We carried thistles, fruit pits, and earth.
We looked to stars in our children's eyes for maps
And sang our best songs of love and rage.

We carried thistles, fruit pits, and earth,
Our money jangled, pocket change.
We sang our best songs of love and rage,
Held creased photographs to our breasts.

Now we carefully count our pocket change,
Sitting at cool tables in basement rooms.
We hold creased photographs to our breasts
As we go to work each day.

We sleep on cool tables in basement rooms
Because we took to the road one cold morning.
As we go to work each day
Fortunes scatter, broken glass across the threshold.

Cuban Missile Crisis

The adults buzz over the t.v.,
over the plastic kitchen radio
over hot black coffee and cigarettes
ringed with bullseyes of red lipstick.

Our Cuban neighbor Horacio
argues with my father
across the kitchen table
across boundaries of language
over the war shadowing us
close above our heads
like the dishtowels we use
to catch my grandmother's
escaped canaries.

Elsa, Horacio's young wife,
crosses her arms in worry.
Newlywed and newly arrived,
she's afraid they've been cast
adrift with no way back,
that her last days will be wasted
in this land of work and strangers.

Another neighbor, Claudina la cubana
clicks her high heels up
and down my parents' hallway
as if the clatter could fill up
the distance between her
and her mother back home.

At school we're ushered
into a windowless hallway,
sit in double rows against walls.

Like when the canaries circle
the room above us,
we're told to cover our heads
with our arms.

Palm Reader

Dip your hands
in sullied
water.

The residue
       of oil
       gushing up
       from the distant ocean floor

       of matted feathers
       of splintered scales

rests in your palms —
a stigmata,
settles into lifelines

foretells a future
I cannot bear
to read.

HOMECOMING, SAN FRANCISCO, 1965

Tono stumbles home loud and late
drops his keys on the pavement
calls up the stairs for Kay, his wife,
to pull the lever, unlock the door.

In the morning she runs a tired hand
through over-permed hair,
lipsticks her crooked teeth
grumbles out the door
to the factory, leaving her old mother
in front of the t.v.

Usually it's just her and her mother
at home over onion sandwiches,
card games, and early nights.

Usually he's out at sea whaling,¯
hunting sperm, humpback and fin
for Del Monte's cat food,
chasing sperm whale oil
for nuclear reactors.

But then he returns,
a broken vessel of a man
with a dream-shattering voice
listing in the late night breeze.

She bides her sleep-deprived time
until his next departure
when man-eaters will again
circle his ship.

MY FATHER COMES HOME FROM WORK

My father comes home from work
sweating through layers of bleached cotton t-shirts
sweating through his wool plaid shirt.

He kisses my mother
starching our school dresses
at the ironing board,

swings his metal lunchbox
onto the formica kitchen table
rattling the remnants
of the lunch she packed
that morning before daylight:

crumbs of baloney sandwiches,
empty metal thermos of coffee,
cores of hard red apples
that fueled his body through
the packing and unpacking of sides
of beef into the walk-in refrigerators
at James Allen and Sons Meat Packers.

He is twenty-six.
Duty propels him each day
through the dark to Butcher Town
where steers walk streets
from pen to slaughterhouse.

He whispers *Jesus Christ*
to no one in particular.
We hear him — me,
my sister Linda, my baby brother Willy,
and la cubana's daughter Mercedes,

who my mother babysits.
When he comes home
we have to be quiet.

He comes into the dark living room.
Dick Clark's American Bandstand
lights my father's face
white and unlined
like a movie star's.
His black hair is combed
into a wavy pompadour.

He sinks into the couch,
takes off work boots
thick damp socks,
rises to carry them
to the porch.

Leaving the room
he jerks his chin toward
the teen gyrations on the screen,
says, *I guess it beats carrying*
a brown bag.

He pauses
for a moment
to watch.

BEAUTY SLEEPING

Beauty is 14
so sleep eludes her
like a lost housecat.

Her dreams are haunted
by Beasts who in a blink
would snatch a girl
on the way home from school.

So Beauty casts spells
with baggy pants, black lipstick, running shoes,
but all the girls know these tricks
and still the front pages scream
the bones of factory girls in the desert.
Girls still disappear into clouds
of dust and the screech of tires
and some Beasts even appear
at a girl's bedside in the night
pretending to be princes.

True, there are those who escape:
girls whose hairclips enchant
car trunk locks,
insomniac girls who hold vigil
until the Beast sleeps
then grab for keys,
girls who kick,
who take the knife
into their own strong hands.

At night Beauty resolves
to be one of these girls,
then checks every lock in the house,

counts the sleeping heads of her parents
and of her seven useless brothers.
At 2 a.m. Beauty turns
over in bed, wishes
she could sleep
for a hundred years.

Goldilocks

When she was sixteen
She couldn't get away
From that house fast enough.

The closet was too small
And she pushed the edges
Of her childhood bed
Longing for a grown-up life
With no dirty dishes to wash
Or mother to answer to.

She streaked her hair blonde
Found an older boyfriend.
Late nights
Her mother would lie awake
Listening for the sound of his car.

At eighteen
Her belly stretched the limits
Of her denim overalls,
And her family gave her
A hurry-up white wedding.
Toward the end of the reception
The zipper of her gown split
And the next week
She was in maternity clothes.

Suddenly she had it all:
A baby in a teddy bear bib
Drooling into his oatmeal;
A reluctant husband
Going out for a smoke
Just as dinner was ready;

An upstairs apartment
Furnished with hand-me-down chairs
And beds in every size.

But all she could think of
Was her mother's voice,
The little house with its
Sink perpetually full of dishes,
And the small child's bed
Whose confines suddenly looked
Just right.

Little Red

I was young.
What girl doesn't drape
herself in red from head to toe
at some point in life?

Red hair
fading toward peroxide orange
red shoes with Spanish heels
bought second hand.

What did I know
about danger?
I thought I would go
undisturbed like a flame
and that strangers would
step aside in awe.

To me forests full of
snakey paths
and wolves
behind every tree
were the stuff
of children's stories.

All I wanted
was to reach my grandmother:
the safety of the chair
beside her wood-burning stove,
the tortilla hot
from the comal and dripping butter,
her starched red apron creased
from a thousand embraces.

But wolves were waiting
to snatch my basket —
and don't believe the bit
about woodcutters
coming to the rescue,
as least not in the way you've been told.

It was grandmother,
who'd lived her whole life
with a stove to fuel,
and studied the ways of wolves,

who grabbed her axe
beat back the wolf
whose breath puffed like a putrid engine
toward the distance.

When it was over
she wiped it across the front of her apron,
said, *Hija, I'm getting too old for this,*
and laid the axe in my hand.

MEXICAN JENNY

I read about it in the paper — two paragraphs. I have carried that story with me ever since, wanting more, wanting no one to have to be those two stark paragraphs.

Dorothy Allison, *Skin*

MEXICAN JENNY

1.

Girls like me
come from alleys
from dirt floors

from cold kitchens
from one thin blanket.

Girls like me
come from fists
from passing strangers

from wandering fathers
from mothers with one heel
hooked on the bar stool.

Girls like me
come from drought
from war.

2.

When I was a child in Acapulco
I worked for a rich family
sweeping their kitchen
washing their dishes.

One day, after a few nips, the cook,
who was my mother's friend,
had said, *Come, work for me*
in the big house.

I stood on a wooden box
washed dishes stamped with indigo
trees and flowers, with birds
like none I'd seen.

I stood elbow
deep in dirty water, dreamed
of far places without greasy pans
nor the boss's wandering hands.

3.

The boss's wife had a red
silk shawl embroidered
with many-colored swallows.
She draped it like a flag on the back of her chair.

It had come on a ship from Manila,
from that land of ship builders and sailors,
of travelers who, years before, brought
Chinese porcelain and silk to Acapulco.

Every time I walked by
I fingered its edges
and felt like I was dipping my fingers
into the tide.

After I'd found the fault lines
in one cup too many,
when I'd daydreamed one
dish too many to pieces,

the cook ran me off,
but not before I'd pinched that shawl,
wrapped it around my waist
under my dirty skirt.

Running home
the silk rubbed
my legs,
a river current.

That's when I took to the road,
the shawl with swallows
darting between thin trees
stuffed at the bottom of my morral.

In 1907, I crossed
the narrow border
that intersects splintering sidewalks
of faded towns.

If I'd known I'd left my country
I'd have crossed myself
as I passed from one land
to the other.

4.

Men's quick fingers are dangerous
as lit dynamite
but I was a snake
and slipped through.

Sometimes I dressed as a boy
in too-big shirts,
in trousers yanked
from backyard clotheslines,
in boots snatched from just inside
back porch doors.

I stole what I did not find.
When I had to, I worked.

I traveled to a land
named in my language
that travelers pointed to
with crooked fingers: *Colorado.*

In my mind it was paved in red velvet
and hibiscus flowers.

But when I got to those gold mining towns
I found dust,
tubercular coughs
ragged men buried daily in the mines
and women whose every mouthful depended
on what was brought to the surface.

5.

I hung gray sheets
in the muddy yard
of one of the best whorehouses
in Cripple Creek.

I heard his step on the gravel
saw his slim outline
cut a dark slit
into the bright morning.

I could not tell
if he was man, woman,
or coyote standing on hind legs.
I could not see his eyes

nor the plans he'd made
before he even saw my face.

6.

Seeing the sun on my black hair
he said, *Cariño, amorcito*
and a handful of other words
held out like breadcrumbs
in his pocketful of New Orleans Spanish.

He must have learned
these words in a song,
but they were enough
to coax me
from my frayed calico dress.

In the street, el pueblo spit
that I was una hija de la mala vida,
but a bad life
was the only life I'd ever known.

7.

I stopped working.
We slept together
in a clapboard rooming house,
ate downstairs with other boarders.

Nights he wrapped his arms
around my body,
pinned my legs with his,
as if I might fly away.

When the landlady looked
at me slant-eyed across the table
and counted under her breath
each tortilla I put onto my plate,
I realized he hadn't paid the rent.
My gut swirled, full of feathers and claws.

8.

Look, he said one day, *you can work for me*
or I go back down that mine shaft.
In a year, maybe two,
we'll be back in the same fix:

I'll be dying, or crippled,
if not dead, and you'll still have to turn tricks
but I won't be strong enough
to protect you.

He said it to me like that.
He promised it would be easy,
that we'd grow fat and rich,
that it wouldn't be work at all.

We lined up at the Justice of the Peace.
In front of us, a pregnant woman
with a bruise across one eye
stood arm-in-arm with a man reeking of whiskey.

He married me and I became Jenny.
Only a few people here could utter the sounds
of my birth name: Genoveva,
and I'd left that old self far away.

He bought me a red velvet dress,
and I began working out of a crib on Meyers Street,
with a narrow bed, a wooden crate
an oil lamp painted with hibiscus flowers.

The men called me
Mexican Jenny
because there were so many Jennys,
girls like me.

9.

It's the Same

Once in awhile a girl
asks what it's like
to earn money
the way I do.

I say it's the same as being married.
When they want it
you give in or risk
a twisted arm or a punch.

You let them do it
to claim a roof,
a meal you cook yourself,
the wool for a winter coat.

It can be sweet with boys
fresh to the mines,
or with older men,
grateful to touch a woman
and willing to pay.

The drunks are the worst
when their bravado sags
into gasping snores.

I steal from them,
balance against the ones
who do their business
then refuse to pay.

I could chase these johns into the street
but that would mean
black eyes
broken teeth,

the same as my husband gives me
when the money doesn't add up
at the end of the night.

10.

I locked everything
that happened
deep underground

but the bullet
and the jail cell
bore into my heart.

Out spilled
a sky black
as crows' wings.

When I started that life
I never saw this end.

11.

Jenny's Mug Shot

To the historian
her defiant smile
means she was confident
she wouldn't be convicted,

that she thought
her story would be believed.

He came at me
like so many other times
because the money
didn't add up.

It was Christmas Day.
He was drunk.
He said he would kill her
but she grabbed the gun.

The sounds of blows,
curses, and broken furniture
were nothing new in Poverty Gulch.
No one came at the blast
just as they hadn't come before.

For the second time in her life
she took flight,
headed for the train,
waited for the connection to El Paso.

On New Year's Eve,
they found his body coated
with a sheen of ice
but her trail was not yet cold.

12.

They say I lied about my age.
They say he was my third husband.
They say I believed I'd get away.

They'll tell you he beat me up
like so many other times
when the money didn't add up.

They'll tell you I shot Phillip Roberts Jr.,
a sometimes blacksmith,
on Christmas Day, 1912.

They'll tell you on New Years Eve
his frozen body was found
face down in our cabin in Poverty Gulch.

They'll say I ran,
that Sherriff Henry Von Phul
discovered I'd bought

a coach ticket to El Paso,
but that the train was delayed,
and he tracked me.

They even say I swam the Rio Grande
into Mexico, though that kind of entrance
has never been necessary.

They say
I joined Pancho Villa's
camp followers.

Von Phul says he found me
at the Capital Hotel in Ciudad Chihuahua,
two-hundred and fifty miles from the border.

He says I greeted him warmly,
and did not resist
arrest.

He says I volunteered
to walk across the border
and meet him on the other side

He says I believed
I would be found innocent
on grounds of self defense.

They're not ashamed to say Von Phul
recruited Billy Dingman, a fugitive
wanted in Cripple Creek,

to help bring me back.
In exchange,
the file on his case disappeared.

It was more important to bring back
a prostitute who'd killed her pimp,
a wife who'd killed her husband.

They wrote *murderess*
across the top
of my mug shot.

I got life
for first degree murder.

13.

Jenny's Alternate Lives

I was born in Colorado,
grew up in Walsenburg.
My mother was Mexican,
my father, German.

I was happy.
I was a runaway.
I loved the touch of man
more than anything.

When I was arrested,
I said Mrs. O'Connor was my mother
and that she lived in Cripple Creek
on East Warren Avenue.

If these things are true,
how did I know the way
to El Paso, and from there
to Ciudad Chihuahua?

How did a girl
who'd never been outside Colorado
know how to get on that train?
How did I know where to go?

14.

Photo of the Sewing Workshop
at the Colorado State Penitentiary
in Cañon City, Colorado

Three women in the foreground
pause at their work
stare into the camera lens.

One leans her chin
on her hand,
mocks a gesture of leisure.

Perhaps forty women sit
over industrial-sized spools.
Half the women sitting straight-backed

over the needle, over long tables,
over sewing machines —
hand cranks and treadles — are Black.

They stitch
shirts and work pants
for male prisoners

because when men are taken
to the whipping post, the Old Grey Mare,
the beating shreds their pants seats.

The women stitch
long plain gowns for the hospital ward,
white cotton aprons for the kitchen workers.

They sew the long canvas dresses
men are forced to wear
when the guards find them fucking.

There are always scraps from this kind of work.
Selvages can be pieced into pillow tops,
pin cushions, small hemmed towels.

Table runners with a few French knots
can be sold to tourists
in the prison gift shop.

In the background of the photo,
men stand against the walls.
Maybe they handled the scissors,

snipped thread, cut yardage
to keep scissors out
of the inmates' sleeves,

out of their cells
where they might use them
against the guards' wandering hands.

The needle is never a threat.
Small and inconspicuous,
its sharpness isn't considered deadly.

Ubiquitous as air
no one would suspect
what a needle might do.

15.

Prisoner 7178: Cañon City, Colorado

I came to the prison with nothing,
but after the trial
bright fabrics from my working
clothes: deep blue, rosa mexicana,
the pale gold of the wings of golondrinas,
were piles of fire in my cell.

When I learned to sew in the prison workshop,
other women gave me clippings
from their own finery.
Little by little I dismantled those dresses
into scraps that told my story,
beginning with flor de jamaica,
with swallows, and butterflies
with a jungle of bougainvillea and trumphet vines.

16.

In the workroom, a girl
hands me the needle saying:
They're called crazy quilts.

They can be any crazy thing
you can think of, nothing is straight or even.
Those patches were the fractured walkway of my life.

I had a great desire
to rip everything
at the weak points.

I took my work clothes
and ripped them to ribbons
saved bright patches near seams,

velvet trims from waistbands and collars
calico bouquets of yellow roses
ruffles that had swept the streets of Cripple Creek.

In the workroom,
after each day's sewing was done,
the same girl taught me lazy daisy, fern, and fly stitch.

I decorated those crooked paths
laced them with blues, whites and greens
with colors of running water.

17.

My Cell

There is one narrow window
higher than my sight line.
A ticking of moldy straw,

covers my plank bed.
In one corner a bucket
leaks onto the floor.

I keep my needle, threads,
the scraps I tear,
folded into a handkerchief.

I have a leather thimble
improvised from the sole
of a worn-out shoe.

I make my own panorama
under a stone-grey sky
dark with sparrows' wings.

I invent flowers,
dogs, and horses
to replace the ones I knew.

I cut a swallow in mid-flight
from the tattered red silk shawl
and appliqué it to a bright blue patch.

I outline shards with fly stitch
so I can soar
out the stone window frame.

I embroider fans to cool the close air of the cell.
I make bullion stitch because I am mining gold
from the dirt of my life.

I embroider his face
over a black velvet patch, hem him in
with rows and rows of feather stitch.

18.

After six winters, I got sick.
The cough shook me through the night
and in 1920, when I coughed blood
onto an apron I was sewing, I was paroled.

The warden sold the quilt in the prison gift shop.
I could be released, but Cripple Creek,
and even Denver, were not safe
from a dangerous woman like me.

I was sorry to see the quilt go,
but the money bought me
a train ticket to El Paso,
then on to Ciudad Chihuahua.

What could I do
but go back to the life,
sick as I was?

I died turning tricks in Mexico,
home or not,
it's where I was buried.

19.

Maybe

The warden came for the quilt
and people who had been friends: neighbors,
working girls, bar men, bought tickets
twenty-five cents each,
because they wanted the quilt, but also
because they wanted me to have a fresh start.

The quilt was displayed
in the prison gift shop.
Even fine people came to see it,
to buy tickets and dream of my quilt
on their parlor tables
over the backs of their upholstered chairs.

Some came because they believed
justice had not been done in my case.
As they slid their quarters
like wishes across the wooden counter,
they remembered mothers, sisters, friends
beaten blue, even killed.

Some thought of me as a soiled dove
like those in the books and newspapers
and believed their money attached them
to the borders of my story.

The quilt was raffled,
I got on the train.
The platform was full of well-wishers.

20.

Other Possibilities

They never knew it, but I got off the train in El Paso,
that being as good a place as any.

I recovered in the dry desert air
and made my living as a seamstress.

There were many more quilts
embroidered with herons,

with storks, and pelicans.
In the end, I missed the first quilt less and less.

Every day I walk past the river,
like me, a moving thing from far away.

Who knows where the current will take me.
Who knows how it ends.

ARS DOMESTICA / ART OF THE NATIVE

RECIPE: HINTERLAND TAMALES

I have never been able to match …
[my mother's] nopales, but I have inherited
her capacity for invention.

— *Helena Maria Viramontes*

Here in Humboldt we have one Mexican market,
El Pueblo, and as the proprietor María says,
at Christmas, todo el mundo comes
to get their masa for tamales.

But I'm inventive and don't want
to drive to the other side of Eureka
to get masa trucked all the way
from San José before daylight.

I make my own masa *almost*
the same way the old ladies
before me have done.
You can do this too.

Go to the market.
The most agavachado chain
grocery, even in the hinterlands
of Aztlán, will have masa harina in bags.

Don't be a baby. Follow the directions
on the back of the bag, behind the face
of ese viejo canoso, that old white haired man
who has no clue as to the contents of that bag.

There's no excuse, honey.
They even print the directions in English.
The trick, though, is in the machinery.

Don't whine about authenticity.
If your grandma had a food processor
you *know* she would've used it.
Deep down, it's the twin sister
of the metate, the molcajete.

No seas mensa, pues.
Wherever the diaspora has flung you and yours
dust off your food processor and make
tamales with masa fresquesita.

Once you have masa, your possibilities
are endless: traditional tamales de puerco,
de pollo en chile verde, de dulce con raisins, or even,
if you're daring, vegetarian tamales
with only God knows what.

Anímate. It's Christmas. All over Aztlán,
just as it's been doing for 500 years,
la tradición continues
to shape shift.

LADY BOUNTIFUL

I am a woman who loves morning,
who rises to dish out
cat food
bird food
fish food.

Like Lady Bountiful,
I dispense nutrition
to all creatures,
then I feed myself,
lace hot milk with
black coffee,
give myself the sweet
with the bitter
in preparation for day.

Could I quit this job?
Could I get up and ignore the hungry cats
circling my feet like whirlwinds?
Could I turn my blind eye
to the fish suckling the surface
of the aquarium?
to the canary hopping
to the low perch
next to the cup of hulls?

Could I rise deaf
to all this?
Could I make myself
pancakes swimming in maple syrup?
Could I go back to bed
licking my fingers
for more?

NOTE TO THE OWNER OF THE RESTAURANT WHERE MY DAUGHTER WORKS

Maybe
when you call her
Dolores
You see the aura
of my mother
María Dolores

Or perhaps you see
other Doloreses who've washed
chopped or stirred,
who've rolled out pasta
in your restaurants.

But I named her
María Allegra
so that she'd run quickly
from sorrow.

She's worked for you
for nine months.
Learn her name.

ABUELA

Before cooking, she'd bless the pots
make the sign of the cross over each empty vessel:
her prayer for enough,
her miracle of multiplication.

Make the sign of the cross over empty vessels,
she whispers to me each cold dawn.
A miraculous multiplication
defied the tyranny of division.

I tell myself each cold dawn:
Live in grandmother's worn path.
In the face of the tyranny of division,
I light candles at the feet of saints.

To live in grandmother's worn path
I plant yerbabuena at each house where I live.
I light candles at the feet of saints
wear an old woman's shoes.

I plant yerbabuena at each house where I live:
in pots on the balcony, in coffee cans in windows.
I wear an old woman's shoes,
rise early to savor a waning darkness.

Pots on the balcony, coffee cans in the window —
these were her prayers for enough.
I rise early to savor a waning darkness.
Before cooking, I bless the pots.

COOKING MENUDO

I.

The meat would come wrapped in pink paper
like a gift for a princess.
Mother tore it open
and would rate it at first glance:
was the layer of crumbly fat too thick?
was it hairy?
had the butcher put in enough
tender honeycomb?

Father's job was to sharpen
the many knives
that the cutting would dull
and to trim the fat.
Then we'd sit
cutting the menudo into squares
the size of a man's thumb,
our hands getting colder and colder,
until it stood heaped
like a pile of white stones.

All the pieces went into the biggest enamel pot,
floated like stars in a dark blue sky.
Then Mother added la pata, cow's hoof,
cut into pieces and smelling of pasture,
along with onions and garlic.

It would cook half the night
then Father would get up at dawn
to turn on the stove and cook it some more.

When she got up, Mother opened cans of nixtamal,
yellow cans of Las Palmas chile
marked on the sides "mild," "medium" or "hot."
She stirred them in with the biggest spoon.

It was alchemy: in the morning steaming bowls would greet us.
We'd roll corn tortillas sprinkled with salt into tight wands.
Over each bowl, we inhaled the scent of our dreams.
Like magicians, we read both past and future
in shiny dregs at the bottoms of our bowls.

II. *Dinner With Julia*

We're lined up on the cracked vinyl couch
waiting like soup kitchen clients
for Julia Child to light up
our living room
with her mannish hands,
her schoolgirl squeals.

We're waiting to see Julia cleave
slabs of meat
and dump the scraps on the floor.
She always sticks her fingers in the food
and then puts them in her mouth.
She's sweaty and disheveled as a saint
before a vision of God.
We're waiting to witness her rapture.

Today Julia hauls bolts of tripe
in ascending sizes from off-camera.
White fields of fat and muscle,
blankets of honeycomb —
only Julia would choose these pieces
as huge as winding sheets for the dead.

We've never seen a woman
handle so much meat
and as casually as if she were
unfurling towels for the clothes line.

And menudo, of all things,
a la française, who was to know
that anyone but us Mexicans

craves tripe, which, when cooked,
fogs the house with its sweaty smell for days.

My mother clucks her tongue.
La Julia is carving the tripe
into squares the size of hands.

My father howls through his
tumbler of red wine,
says, *She must be drunk,*
tossing those dirty plates
off-screen without a thought.

But we all love Julia,
wait weekly to see her,
a broad-shouldered
square-bodied woman
who cooks with both hands
up to her elbows in the food
and opens her mouth all the way
to laugh.

SUNDAY MORNING

You come to the table,
plates piled with French toast:
last night's
sesame
bread
laced with egg, studded with cinnamon,
adorned with medallions
of banana,
with golden slivers
of pear.

You pop
the lid on
the syrup
and hand it to me first, saying,
It could be worse,
it has been worse.

I take a bite, give you
a syrupy kiss
and shout,
Amen.

WHAT WE ATE AT MY GRANDMOTHER'S HOUSE

Chicken fricassee
Beans and posole

Chiles rellenos
Chicken and dumplings

Macaroni and cheese
Tortillas de harina
Hechas a mano
Sonora style
Big as the map of the world.

COLOR SNAPSHOTS

1993
My daughter Allie's hair is dark brown. When she stands in the sun I see individual strands of burgundy. Except for the highlights, her hair and mine are the same color.

1968
A stranger asks my grandma Sofia if she's Indian. *Oh no*, she answers quickly, *I'm Mexican.*

1971
In the seventh grade, my cousins Rico Hernandez and Dawn McGuigan are in the same class as my sister, Linda. She stands up and explains to the class how exactly they are related.

1977
During his low-rider youth, my blond cousin Mark tells his parents he wants to dye his hair black.

1992
My mother-in-law only buys Allie blond dolls. Until I start to get noticeably gray, I stop lightening my hair.

2000
At my son's school, another mother asks which child is mine. I tell her Alex is my son. She smiles and says, *I must not know him, the only Alex I know is Oriental.*

1997
After seeing us together, a classmate in my daughter's new school asks her if she's adopted. She asks every day.

2001
I'm in line at the post office. A woman lines up behind me and notices two red-haired boys playing on the floor in the corner. She eyes my red hair, and then concludes, *Oh, they must be yours.*

1982
A stranger stops me on the street in Oakland, asks if I'm Eurasian.

1992
I'm standing in the patio of my daughter's pre-school when a mexicana picks me out of the crowd to ask for directions in Spanish.

1942
During my mother's childhood, her father's name of endearment for her is india fea.

1971
We look at my grandfather Luis' Mexican national identity card. Under *raza* it is clearly marked *mestizo.* My uncle Louie is surprised.

1927
My grandmother María sends her brothers Denisio and José to pick up her daughter Margarita from school. They accidentally bring home another child, una americanita. When they show up at the door with the wrong child, my grandmother hurls curses at their backs as they hurry away to exchange the children and bring my aunt home.

1992

My daughter is four, and suddenly aware of her own color. *Why do I have to be brown?* she laments. *Because people usually look like the others in their family,* I reply, confident I've come up with a reassuring answer. She eyes me, exasperated that I've missed the point, and wails, *But you're white!*

1990

I'm going through the grocery checkout. The clerk eyes my son and chirps, *Oh, your husband must be Chinese.*

1991

Allie's pre-school teacher asks if her father Tony is Native American. *No,* I say, *we're Mexican.*

1966

My dad won't let my mother pierce our ears because, he says, it would make my sister and I look like gypsies.

2000

Rachael my hairdresser says that with light hair I'm a dead ringer for Julio Iglesias's first wife.

1905

At age five, my grandma Sofía travels from Tucson to Hermosillo, Sonora, Mexico by wagon train. She meets her great grandmother, who, although she is an old lady, is a blond with sparkling blue eyes. She is tiny as a doll and owns orchards that stretch for miles.

1940
Everyday, Lucille, my grandfather Bill's sister, passes the house
where he lives with my grandma Sofía. Lucille disapproves
of her white Texan brother's life with my Arizona Mexican
grandmother. She refuses to visit them.

1997
I tell Allie that people who think that all members of a family
have to be the same color have no imagination.

1988
When she's six weeks old, I take Allie to the doctor and he
pierces her ears.

To the Spoon

Oh spoon, mouth-sized receptacle,
cupped hand, you offer sustenance
one swallow at a time.

Smallest sister to the bowl
cousin to the plate,
you deliver medicine,
bitter tastes in tiny sips.

Soup spoon, purveyor of one taste,
then two.
Demitasse spoon hiding
at the back of the drawer
until called on to feed
visiting babies who kick with glee.

Silver spoon tarnished
like an old relative
I polish up for the holidays,
stainless steel serving spoon
bright as a smart daughter,
straight-postured as a robust son.

Teaspoon circumnavigating the hot cup
until unlike forms are wedded into one.
Ladle like a pregnant sister
expanding the family's wealth.

Dessert spoon cupping sweetness
like a lover's breast,
measuring spoons nesting
like a loving family.

Oh, spoon, you deliver
the last gulps of this life
to our parched lips.

Teach us to serve
with our whole bodies
to feed the world

then to rest side by side
in a delectable embrace.

7 Stanzas About Rum

for Red Shuttleworth

6 candles illuminate
rum cake with pineapple filling.
My grandmother
pops open a beer.

◆ ◆ ◆

When I turn 21
my boyfriend takes me to Trader Vic's:
chunks of sweet deep fried chicken
 a rum drink with an umbrella.

◆ ◆ ◆

Mojitos with freshly crushed mint
on a summer evening
in Tony and Cecilia's back yard:
a sleepy ride back home.

◆ ◆ ◆

My souvenirs of Puerto Rico:
photos of myself
in a jíbaro's straw hat
eyes half closed.

◆ ◆ ◆

Puerto Vallarta
for honeymoon #1
an empty coconut
poolside.

◆ ◆ ◆

Puerto Vallarta for honeymoon #2
(different husband)
empty glasses on the sea wall
remind me I've been here before.

◆ ◆ ◆

Oh, full bottle under the kitchen sink, shelter
this tart heart on sugared summer evenings,
on winter nights
when spirits come calling.

SATURDAY FROM MY SECOND STORY WINDOW

The top of a clear-cut hill
A stand of cypress trees

Earnest neighbors with wheelbarrow and shovel
An armchair adorns another neighbor's driveway

The gray roof of the Methodist church
The concrete building where I work

Three fluttering sparrows
A ragged-winged turkey vulture
gliding, gliding.

TYING MY SHOES

I tie my shoes
bend to draw them tight
brace myself
for each hard step
of this day.

I tie the laces slowly
like I did when, at five,
I first memorized this rite.

The crossed laces mean:
bless the bones of my feet.

The knot means tendons
anchor me to this life.

Each bow loop
forms one ear of the cow
whose hide made these shoes.

Bending low
I whisper into each ear
hail holy earth
blessed art thou
creation.

1976, STOCKTON, CALIFORNIA: WITH GLORIA IN THE CORN

We were so young
our womanhood
glowed green and as hard
as the corn growing all around us.

We drove to the field
in someone's big car:
Rene, Olivia,
Gloria and I,
and others whose names
time has snatched back
from my memory.

The car fogged up
with giggling breath.
Our laughter jingled like money
as we sat thigh-to-thigh
in the hot valley night.
The land echoed voices in wet
whispers across a purple dusk.

Stopped at the side
of the road,
we spilled a jumble
of legs into the pitch.

We felt our way in the dark
reached for hardly yellow corn,
laughed as we slipped it
into pockets improvised
from skirt fronts.

Completely blind,
I read the whole world with my hands
until Gloria touched my face,
whispered, *look, a shooting star.*

A halo arced
over the corn.

In the afterglow
we were bright stalks
tender as hands
in darkness.

NOTES

"HOMECOMING: SAN FRANCISCO, 1965"

The old upstairs Victorian flats in San Francisco had mechanical levers at the top of the interior staircases so one could open the front door without walking down the stairs. Also, although some sources mark the end of Pacific coast whaling at the early 20th century, there was a resurgence of whaling out of the San Francisco Bay after World War II that continued until the passage of the Marine Mammal Protection Act of 1972 (baynature.org). (During this period, whale meat was used to make commercial dog and cat food, and sperm whale oil was sold to the nuclear industry as a lubricant used in the production of weapons and electricity.)

"MEXICAN JENNY"

I discovered the story of Jenny Wenner, a.k.a. Mexican Jenny, years ago in a back issue of *Piecework*, a textile arts magazine. The article announced a quilt exhibit that included a crazy quilt Jenny made in the 1920s, when she was incarcerated at the prison in Cañon City, Colorado.

According to the article, Jenny had been a prostitute in Cripple Creek, a gold mining town, and she killed her husband "with his own gun" after he beat her up for not bringing home enough money. She was convicted of murder, and in prison made a quilt from her working girl clothes, complete with the embroidered image of her dead husband. When she contracted tuberculosis in prison, the quilt was sold and the money used to send her to Mexico "where she spent her last days."

This story haunted me. I wanted to know who this woman was, what brought her to Colorado, and what brought her into "the life." Over the years, I made a few efforts at researching her story and found no record of her. Finally, I used the original bare bones of this story and began to flesh it out with my own imaginings.

72

Because Jenny was sent to Mexico at the end of her life, I created a Mexican early life for her, and motives that would lead her to Colorado. When I was writing the part of poem about her time in Cripple Creek, I researched the lives of prostitutes in western mining towns and ran across Jan MacKell's book *Brothels, Bordellos, & Bad Girls: Prostitution in Colorado 1860-1930*. MacKell has a 4-page account of the case of Jennie Wenner, (different spelling) which gave me various facts of the case, including a dramatic mug shot in which Jennie defiantly looks into the camera's lens, and two more sedate prison photos. Some of the details from MacKell's account contradicted my own story: like the revelation that Jennie was born in Colorado. Others gave me a timeline to work with: she killed her husband on Christmas night, 1913, and entered prison in May of the next year. MacKell also relates that Sherriff Von Phul of Cripple Creek pursued Jennie to Ciudad Chihuahua, Mexico, and apprehended her with the assistance of a fugitive from the law. Some facts of Jennie's case are woven into my poem, and others she disputes in her own voice. Because of these conflicts of fact, folklore and interpretation, I have given her story three different endings and it's told in multiple voices.

A photograph of a sewing workshop in the prison is referenced in the poem: this photograph is published in Sandra Dallas's *The Quilt that Walked to Golden: Women and Quilts in the Mountain West*. The same photo, and other details about the prison are included in *Prisons of Cañon City* by Victoria R. Newman and the Museum of Colorado Prisons.

"COLOR SNAPSHOTS"
The form for this poem was inspired by Deborah Harding Allbritain's poem "How I Knew Harold," published in Steve Kowits's, *In the Palm of Your Hand*.

ABOUT THE AUTHOR

Barbara Brinson Curiel is a native of San Francisco, California. She has recently published poems in the journals: *Kweli, Huizsache,* and *The Acentos Review,* as well as in the chapbook anthology, *Mirage.* Her poems are included in the 2011 collection *Cantar de Espejos: Poesía Testimonial Chicana por Mujeres* published in Mexico, and in anthologies including: *Under the Fifth Sun: Latino Literature From California; The Floating Borderlands: Twenty-five Years of U.S. Hispanic Literature; and, Literatura Chicana 1965-1995.*

Barbara's first book of poetry, *Speak to Me From Dreams,* was published in 1989 (Third Woman Press). She published two chapbooks: *Nocturno,* and *Vocabulary of the Dead,* early in her writing career. Her 2010-2012 fellowship with CantoMundo, the national organization for Latino poets, has fostered a renewed period of writing and publishing after a hiatus devoted to family and career.

A graduate of Mills College, Stanford University, and with a Ph.D. from the University of California, Santa Cruz, Barbara is a professor in the departments of Critical Race, Gender, and Sexuality Studies and English at Humboldt State University, where she teaches creative writing, Chicano/Latino and feminist studies, and American literature. She has published scholarly essays on the narrative writings of Latina authors. Barbara is also a textile artist.